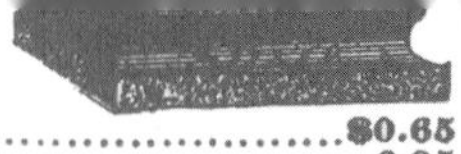

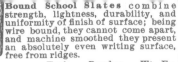

...nly, very durably
...e. Weight, packed, 4
...ces. Each 6c.
...r doz $0.65
...r gross 6.95

53510 The Matchless Dustless Eraser, made of thin fancy colored felt, firmly secured, forming a substantial and perfect eraser.
Each........ $0.05
...r doz.... .55
...r gross........ 5.45

...uth's Companion and Reversible Blackboard.

...512 Combination ...ting and Drawing ...k. Suitable for ...e, Sunday and ...ate schools. Both ...s slated, hard wood ...e. 3 feet 11 inches ..., 2 feet wide. The ... complete, perfect ...reliable black board ...e. Price..... $3.00

Portable Black-Boards.

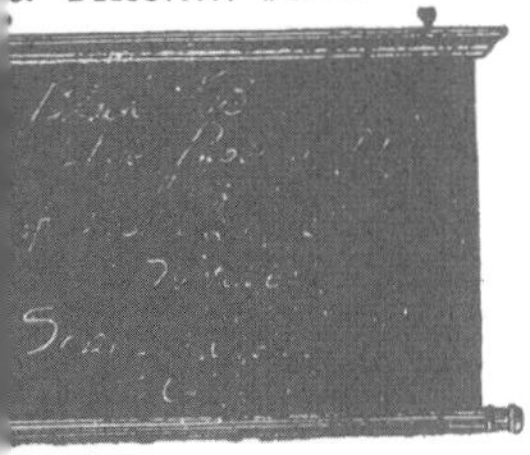

53514 Portable Blackboard of cloth with best black liquid slating surface on both sides, mounted on rollers with hook and rings complete ...anging.

Size.	Each.	Size.	Each.	Size.	Each.
...t.	$0 54	3x5 ft.	$1 90	4x5 ft.	$2 30
...t.	1 14	3x6 ft.	2 30	4x6 ft.	2 85
...t.	1 50	4x4 ft.	1 90	4x7 ft.	3 30

...th music lines, $1.25 each, additional.

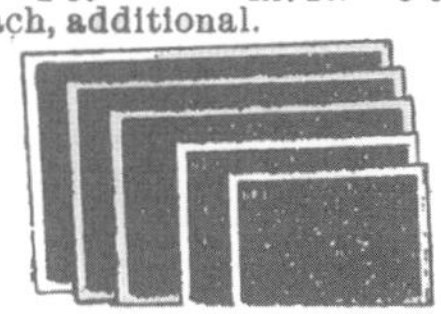

...516 Portable ...ckboard of Hylo...e, slated both sides; ... ash frame; for ... on wall, easel or ...e.

...t.	$2.60	3½x5	$5.50
...t.	3.60	4 x6	7.15
... ft.	4.55		

...th music lines, $1.25 each additional.
...versible portable blackboards, same as No. ..., mounted on hardwood standards, for private ...ols, Sunday schools, lecture rooms, etc. Prices ... be quoted on application.

Slated Paper and Cloth.

...518 For Blackboard; excellent for any flat ...ace.

	Per yard.
...per, 3 ft. wide, slated one side, black	$0.47
...per, 4 ft. wide, slated one side, black	.60
...520	
...oth, 3 ft. wide, slated one side, black	.54
...oth, 4 ft. wide, slated one side, black	.67
...oth, 3 ft. wide, slated two sides, black	.67
...oth, 4 ft. wide, slated two sides, black	.80

...iquid Slating for Blackboands.

...522 Best Alcohol Black Liquid Slating; may

Bound School Slates combine strength, lightness, durability, and uniformity of finish of surface; being wire bound, they cannot come apart, and machine smoothed they present an absolutely even writing surface, free from ridges.

Size.	Each.	Per doz.	Wt., Ea.
6x 9	$0.04	$0.42	18 oz.
7x11	0.05	0.48	22 oz.
8x12	0.06	0.60	25 oz.
6x 9, 12 doz. in case, per case			$4.75
7x11, 10 doz. in case, per case			4.50
8x12, 8 doz. in case, per case			4.50

"Hyatt Noiseless Slates.

53528 Strength, lightness and durability combined. Best quality slate with perfectly finished, even writing surface, free from ridges. Frame is wire bound (cannot come apart) and covered with fine bright red (fast color) wool felt, securely fastened.

"Hyatt" Noiseless Slate, single.

Size.	Each.	Per doz.	Wt., Ea.
6x 9	$0.08	$0.80	18 oz.
7x11	0.10	1.00	23 oz.
8x12	0.12	1.20	26 oz.
6x 9, 12 doz. in case, per case			$9.00
7x11, 10 doz. in case, per case			9.00
8x12, 8 doz. in case, per case			8.40

53529 "Hyatt" Noiseless Slate, double, hinged with strong webbing, firmly riveted to frames.

Size.	Each.	Per doz.	Wt., Ea.
7x11	$0.20	$2.00	40 oz.
8x12	0.24	2.40	46 oz.
7x11, 5 doz. in case, per case			$9.00
8x12, 4 doz. in case			8.40

Victor Slates.

53530 Best Quality Slates, with perfectly smooth surface; frame covered with bright red wool felt and securely fastened.

Size.	Each.	Per doz.
5x7	$0.08	$0.80
6x9	.09	.95
7x11	.10	1.05
8x12	.12	1.25

Silicate Book Slates.

Superior quality, strongly made, bound in fine black cloth covers. Superior slate surface for the slate pencil. For school or office use.

		Size.	Each.
53532	6 surfaces	5x8½	$0.25
	6 surfaces	6x9	.35

Silicate Book Slates, neatly and strongly bound in fine cloth, with superior **ivorine surface, for the lead pencil.** For the pocket.
53534 6 surfaces, size 3x5, each........ $0.15
10 surfaces, size 3¼x5⅛, each........ .25

Scholar's Companions.

53413 Turned Wood Case, fancy paper covered, furnished with slate and lead pencil, pen holder and ruler. Each, 3c; per doz........ $0.30

53415 Unique Scholar's Companion, varnished maple box, with sliding cover, 9-inch ruler attachment with scale, fitted with lead pencil, slate pencil and pen holder. Size, 9x2x1⅛ inches. Each, 8c; per doz........ $0.85

53417 Scholar's Companion, bass wood, shellac finish, 3 compartments each

...ceipts, invoices, letters and memoranda of every description, made from best ...
...inches wide.
Each........ $0.04
Per dozen...... 0.40

53474. "Ever-Handy" Paper Clip, medium size, with jaws ... inches wide. Each.. $0.06 Per doz........ $0...

"Spencerian" Ever-Handy Paper Clip.

53475. "Spencerian" Paper Cl... Horseshoe shape; brass, size 1¾ x ... inches.
Each........ $0...
Per dozen........ 0...

School Bags.

53490. School Bag. Fan... Hemp, embroidered front, wi... pocket; size 11½ x 14 inche... weight packed 5 oz.
Each........ $...
Per doz........ ...

53491. Waterproof School Bag, with outside pocket, shoulder strap and flap, bound edges. Weight packed 5 oz.
Each, 14 in........ $.10
Per doz........ .95
Each, 16 inch........ .12
Per doz........ 1.20

53492. School Bag, ha... cotton cord, closely woven ... variegated colored stripe... lined, cord handles, 14 inche...
Each........ $0.1...
Per doz........ 1...

53493. School Bag, Brown Duck, flap fastens with strap and lock, leather shoulder strap. Size 9½x14. Very durable.
Each........ $0.18
Per doz........ 1.90

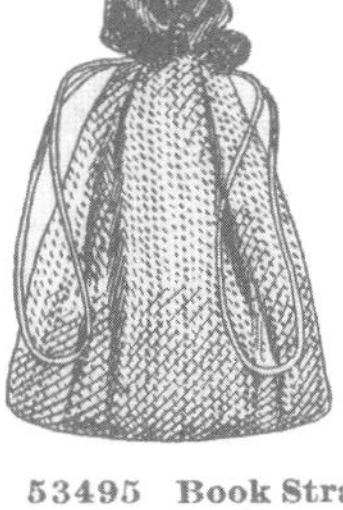

53494 School Bags, cott... cord in variegated colore... stripes, lined with colored cam... bric, with drawing strings, si... when open 14x17½ inches.
Each........ $0.2...
Per dozen........ 2...

53495 Book Straps, flexible leather, handle wi... cross-bars and name plate, 36 inch strap.
Each........ $0.1...
Per doz........ 1...

Education

LIFE IN AMERICA 100 YEARS AGO

Education

Linda Leuzzi

Chelsea House Publishers
Philadelphia

CHELSEA HOUSE PUBLISHERS
Editor-in-Chief: Stephen Reginald
Managing Editor: James D. Gallagher
Production Manager: Pamela Loos
Art Director: Sara Davis
Picture Editor: Judy Hasday
Senior Production Editor: Lisa Chippendale

LIFE IN AMERICA 100 YEARS AGO

Staff for *EDUCATION*
Editorial Assistant: Anne Hill
Designer: Keith Trego
Picture Researcher: Sandy Jones
Cover Illustration: Robert Gerson

First Printing

1 3 5 7 9 8 6 4 2
Library of Congress Cataloging-in-Publication Data

Leuzzi, Linda.
Education / Linda Leuzzi.

p.   cm. — (Life in America 100 Years Ago)
Includes bibliographical references and index.

ISBN 0-7910-2849-6 (hc)
   1. Education—United States—History—19th century. I. Title. II. Series.
LA216.L48   1998
370′.973′09034—dc21   97-27664
                                                                          CIP

CONTENTS

LIFE IN AMERICA 100 YEARS AGO

Communication

Education

Frontier Life

Government and Politics

Health and Medicine

Industry and Business

Law and Order

Manners and Customs

Sports and Recreation

Transportation

Urban Life

Education

How American Education Evolved

THE OLD GOOSETOWN SCHOOL, WHICH WAS BUILT IN NEW York around 1880 and used for primary school classes until the 1930s, is typical of the one-room country schools where many American children prepared for their future a century ago.

And although regular classes have not been held at the Goosetown School for many years, learning does still go on there. The wood-frame school building was moved to nearby Hill-Hold Park and Museum, where visitors can walk inside and see how education was different 100 years ago.

What was the classroom like at the turn of the century? In many cases, grades one to eight were taught in one schoolroom, which could hold about 30 students. To get there, students walked several miles through fields, carrying school books and a piece of coal or wood for the pot-bellied stove, because fuel to heat the school was donated by the community. After stepping through the entryway, the children dropped the fuel into a large bin, and hung their coats and scarves on hooks.

The Goosetown School in New York was used as a one-room schoolhouse for over 50 years. The building was later moved and is now an educational display at the Hill-Hold Park and Museum in New York. The school is similar to most of the schoolhouses where America's youth were taught 100 years ago.

To the left was the classroom, where natural daylight flooded through large windows on three sides of the building. Students read their lessons by this light; there was no electricity, and to compensate for gloomy days, the walls and ceilings were painted white.

By 1900, standard lessons included reading, writing and grammar, arithmetic, history, civics, pronunciation, and geography. Classes in agriculture and nature were also added around this time. Students worked out fractions and decimals, diagrammed sentences, or explained the unique crops, weather, and land of an American state or another country, as they pointed to chalk-drawn shapes on the "blackboard," a wooden board painted black. Students also memorized and recited lessons from textbooks, and choruses of children's voices repeated multiplication tables and the dates of important events throughout the day. A youngster who fell behind might be teamed up with an older classmate. Teachers followed detailed daily schedules and noted each student's progress.

Between 1880 and the 1930s, most American children prepared for their future in one-room schoolhouses. Eventually, however, the one-room country school began to fade from American education as it evolved into the separately-taught grades of today. Bigger new schools were built, accommodating larger classes and more teachers, and transportation improved, drawing more students.

THE ROOTS OF AMERICAN EDUCATION

Formal education for youngsters can be traced as far back as ancient Greece. The first school system established by a government to train its citizens began late in the seventh century B.C. in Sparta, where boys began basic physical training at age seven and girls had their own separate gymnasiums. Today's basic education has its roots in ancient

At the turn of the century, school was taught in small classrooms. Often, students in first through eighth grades were seated together, as are these immigrant children in New York City.

Athens, where students were taught several subjects such as music, reading, writing, arithmetic, and gymnastics.

The schools that American settlers established followed those of 16th-century Europe, where a classical form of education had evolved. The thrust was humanist, offering courses that stimulated the student to become a civic-minded person. The Protestant gymnasium, or the seminary run by the Catholic Jesuits, taught Greek and Latin grammar, morality and religion, and practical subjects through regimented study. This set the overall pattern of education for the next 300 years.

When the Puritans came from Europe in the 1600s, their households became the first schools of the New World and the women of these households were the principal teachers. Puritan law required all children to receive an education. After a town was settled, a school would invariably be built a few years later. For example, Dedham, Massachusetts, was established near Boston in 1636 by about 30 families. A church was formed two years later, and in 1643 a town meeting authorized the first school. The townspeople contributed the schoolmaster's salary each year.

This particular Dedham school was a secondary school. Most students were boys from prosperous families who would later attend college, so the Dedham school offered the subjects taught at European schools. Students learned reading and arithmetic by memorization. The classical subjects, Greek and Latin, were also taught. And the main textbook was the New England Primer, which integrated the Puritans' religious outlook with their education.

As girls weren't admitted to the earliest schools, they might be sent to "dame" schools—informal schools set up in a woman's home—to learn letters and numbers. Outside New England, another opportunity for girls to learn was through apprenticeships. Young girls were sent to

13

A page from the New England Primer, one of the earliest school texts published in America. It was first printed before 1690 and featured moralizing couplets and woodblock illustrations. Over two million copies of the New England Primer were printed during the 18th century.

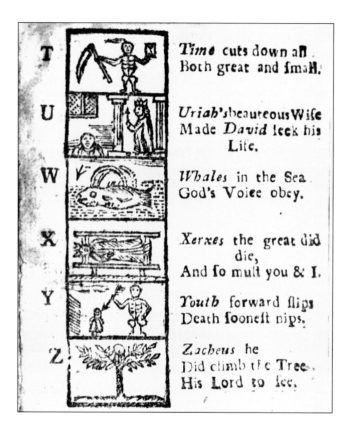

live with another family at a young age, where they might learn reading and household skills.

While educational conditions varied in the early years, there was an attempt to provide standards. Specific guidelines for elementary schools became British law in 1647, and the guidelines were updated in 1692. With this new legislation, towns of 100 or more families had to build schools, keep them operating, and hire teachers.

Later laws to improve teaching standards went further. At that time,

The earliest classes in the American colonies were taught in each town's meeting house until a school could be built. Only boys were taught at these schools—girls learned to read and write at informal dame schools set up in a woman's home.

teachers included ministers, young college graduates, and men who also held other jobs, such as innkeepers or surveyors, because a teaching position was considered a step to a better-paying job. In an attempt to provide a better education, new laws restricted part-time teaching and made it a requirement that each school was to have a certified person who taught Latin. These laws were strictly enforced; records show that Dedham was indicted for not following certain guidelines. By 1755, Dedham had grown to four school systems, and most of its schoolmasters were Harvard graduates.

HIGHER EDUCATION IN THE COLONIES

The first college in the New World, Harvard, was founded in 1636. What sparked the Puritans' need to build schools for higher learning so soon after settling in a primitive new land where everything had to be done by hand? One reason was their beliefs; the Puritans believed everyone should be educated enough to read and consider Scripture and the effect its stories and lessons had on their daily lives.

Several of the Puritan leaders from the Massachusetts Bay Colony were graduates of Cambridge University in England. Cambridge dated to the 12th century, and it provided a liberal arts program that included grammar, rhetoric, and logic, as well as music, arithmetic, geometry, and the study of classical literature. This background gave colonial leaders a reference point for Harvard's curriculum. Two other colonial colleges followed Harvard: the College of William and Mary, founded in Virginia in 1693, and Yale, established in 1701.

Women would not be admitted to college campuses until 1833, when Oberlin College, the first coeducational school, was established in Ohio. However, colonial American women did branch out intellectually. Some Puritan women published their religious thoughts. Quaker

This engraving shows Harvard College as it appeared around 1739. Harvard, located in Cambridge, Massachusetts, was founded in 1636 and was the first college in the New World.

women could preach and run meetings, and eventually schools were created to teach them how to do this. The Moravians, a Christian religious group from Czechoslovakia, began a boarding school for their young women in 1749, and later opened the Moravian Seminary to the public. A girls' school was founded in Philadelphia in 1754, in the same building as the Boys' Latin School. Young women from prosperous families could also attend finishing schools, where they studied music, dancing, literature, and French.

THE GENESIS OF PUBLIC EDUCATION

After the Revolutionary War, America's citizens began rethinking the classroom and debated what courses would help the new country prosper.

In 1785, Congress passed an ordinance requiring every town to reserve land for an elementary school. Although public schools in America dated to the early Dutch settlement of New Netherland, the idea of a tax-supported free school system began to take shape in several states after this time. New York organized the University of the State of New York as a statewide school system in 1784. By 1820, the New York Public School Society had established a network of free public elementary schools for children in the city. In 1821, the first public high school, for boys ages 12 to 15, was opened in Boston, and a school for girls followed five years later. The next year, 1827, Massachusetts required every large town to build a free high school, and in 1837, it became the first state to establish a board of education to set school laws, establish qualifications for teachers, and improve school buildings.

The move toward public education was slow; at first only New England and New York established education for all at the public's

Horace Mann (1796-1859) was one of the pioneers of American public education. While secretary of the Massachusetts Board of Education, he established state-operated schools, set teaching requirements, standardized the curriculum, raised salaries for teachers, and improved schools and equipment. Other states soon followed Massachusetts' example.

SCHOOL FOR COLORED GIRLS

Before the Civil War, there were few opportunities for African Americans to receive an education. Citizens of Canterbury, Connecticut, threatened violence against Prudence Crandall, forcing her to close her academy for black girls in 1833.

expense. Funds for the schools came from lotteries, license fees, fines, and the sale of public lands.

Many people had mixed feelings about the idea of state-supported free public schools in the early 1800s. Some parents felt embarrassed, because to send a child to the public school meant the family couldn't afford private school. Other parents resisted, saying their children were needed to work so the family could survive. Some people believed education for everyone was not necessary because the country was

mainly agricultural, so most work did not require technical training. And some felt public education would encourage laziness by providing a "free ride."

Eventually, however, these ideas began to change, especially in the North and West. More and more immigrants were pouring into the cities, and significant inventions and machinery were becoming part of the American workplace. These new citizens needed some education in order to live and work in this country. Educators like Horace Mann, who had initiated Massachusetts' first board of education in 1837 and established the first state-operated public school in 1839, believed in a common school movement that would remove potential social prejudice by making the same kind of school available to all.

Mann, the first secretary of the Massachusetts School Board, oversaw many changes in public schools throughout the state. His reforms included a minimum six-month school year, state funding for public education, and increases in teacher salaries. His ideas about education spread to other areas, and by 1850 there were about 80,000 primary schools and 300 high schools in the United States.

EDUCATIONAL INJUSTICES

Most African Americans could not attend public schools. Education for African Americans did exist—a black man received a degree from an American university in 1826—but there were few opportunities. Most of the schools that were open specifically for African Americans in the 18th and 19th centuries were religious schools in the North. A handful of southern plantation households taught black children, and southern schools that admitted blacks were run secretly in larger cities.

But educators of both races fought these injustices. In 1793, Katy Ferguson, a former slave who had bought her freedom, established a

21

school in New York open to both poor black and white children. Prudence Crandall, a white teacher in Canterbury, Connecticut, faced many hardships when she admitted an African-American girl to her class in 1832. When the plucky Crandall turned the school into an academy exclusively for African-American girls, the townspeople turned against her and she was arrested and jailed. Eventually, when rocks were thrown through the school windows, Crandall felt she could no longer protect her 20 students and the academy was closed.

Educators like Ferguson and Crandall were among many who led the way in making change possible for blacks. Educational opportunities, while not ideal, did improve; there were 4,000 schools for African Americans by 1870, and by 1876, 40 percent of black children were being educated in southern schools.

Before 1780, there was no written alphabet for the centuries-old Native American languages until a Cherokee named Sequoyah invented 85 characters to represent the sounds of his nation's language. Sequoyah worked on this project for 12 years. By 1823, an estimated 1,000 Cherokee had learned to read and write in their own language.

Mission schools, run by religious organizations, were established specifically for Native Americans during this period. The missions, such as the California schools developed by Catholic Franciscans between 1782 and 1810, aimed to discourage the Native American way of life, to encourage farming and homemaking skills, and to convert students to teachers' religious beliefs. Later, groups like the Quakers made a sincere effort to educate and not convert.

Also, although it was not a widespread policy, tribally controlled education did exist for some Native Americans. The five "Civilized Tribes"—the Cherokee, Creek, Choctaw, Chickasaw and Seminole— asked for educational funding in their treaties with the U.S. govern-

Sequoyah (1766-1843) was a Cherokee Indian who developed a written alphabet for his Cherokee language. A newspaper and parts of the Bible were printed in Cherokee, and Sequoyah taught thousands of Cherokees to read and write.

ment and received it for many decades. While funding did depend on the tribes' relocation west, the federal government gave the Native Americans freedom to select their own teachers for educational, mechanical, and agricultural classes. The Choctaw and Cherokee were the most progressive; between them, the two nations operated over 200 schools and academies. Funds also were set aside to send Native Americans with higher education needs to prestigious colleges.

There were some significant advances toward equality in academics during the latter part of the 19th century. Public high schools numbered 100 in 1860, just before the Civil War; there were 6,000 by 1900 and more than half of all high school graduates were women. There also were compulsory attendance laws in 31 states and territories by 1900. For the next wave of new immigrants pouring into America, free education was a miracle. In their homelands, education was something available only to royalty or to the rich, and most immigrants were eager for their children to take advantage of this opportunity. Teaching, which was initially male-dominated, evolved into a profession mainly for women. Teaching offered less regimentation and fewer hours than factory work. By 1900, almost 75 percent of all teachers were women. Many had long careers and some advanced to top educational positions. Amy Morris Bradley began her 50-year career in a country school in Maine and ended it as superintendent of schools in North Carolina in 1891. Maria Baldwin, an African-American, started as a teacher at the Agassiz School in Cambridge, Massachusetts, in 1881, becoming principal of the nearly all-white school by 1889 and eventually becoming master.

The mother of a well-to-do New York family gets her young daughter ready for school.

Students were taught "The Three R's" (Reading, 'Ritin', and 'Rithmatic) in one-room schoolhouses. Many elementary grades were often taught in one building by the same teacher.

At lunchtime and after school, students played fun games like marbles, tag, or "crack the whip," a game in which the students would grip each other's hands tightly and run across the schoolyard trying to shake each other loose.

A long afternoon of lessons in a country school.

Innovative Educators

IN 1900, OVER 80 PERCENT OF AFRICAN AMERICANS LIVED IN rural areas of the South. However, they suffered from many disadvantages in education, including a short school year and poorly trained teachers. Textbooks, desks, and blackboards were not available, nor were teaching aids, and teachers' salaries were so low they had to be supplemented by black churches.

These schools needed teachers who could compensate for the many inequities, and Fanny Jackson Coppin, the first African American to graduate from Oberlin College, made sure some of these schools got them. Coppin headed the Institute for Colored Youth in Philadelphia—now known as Cheyney University—from 1869 until 1902. She initiated programs to train teachers, preparing her students so thoroughly they could teach from memory. Students at the Quaker-run school learned drawing and map making so they could produce illustrations for their own classes. They were lectured on health, school hygiene, and preventive medicine by a physician, because most southern students lived miles away from medical doc-

tors, and the Institute teachers were expected to steer students toward a healthier lifestyle.

Coppin, a freed slave, knew the difficulties Institute teachers would encounter in the South, and she explained the conditions to her classes. Yet she encouraged Institute graduates to teach in those schools even though the pay was lower.

While educators like Coppin were finding ways to provide better opportunities for African Americans, Native Americans were struggling to do the same for themselves. Although the five Civilized Tribes ran their own schools until 1915, most Native Americans counted on the government for education. Tutoring and schooling for Native Americans was initiated on a widespread basis by the government in 1870. At the time, President Ulysses S. Grant recommended that vacated agencies on Indian reservations be filled by people nominated by religious organizations. This meant ministers or missionaries with strong religious beliefs were charged with educating—and in many cases, converting—the "heathen" natives.

By the late 1870s, off-reservation boarding schools were suggested as a solution to educate Native Americans. In theory, the schools would introduce Native Americans to American culture so they could compete for jobs. However, there were several problems with the plan. The boarding schools separated the youngsters from their families and communities for long stretches of time, and the culture the Native American youths knew was discouraged by the schools.

Sarah Winnemucca, a feisty, passionate Paiute, felt there should be a better way to educate her people. Winnemucca had taught herself English and served as a translator for the U.S. Army. An eloquent

By 1900, educational opportunities for African Americans were becoming more available. However, teachers needed to be trained to cope with limited funds and resources.

Education

speaker, she championed the rights of her people, who had been forced from their land in Nevada, and she once met with President Rutherford B. Hayes about abuses the tribe suffered under corrupt Indian agents. She met many prominent people in her quest to fight injustices, including Elizabeth Palmer Peabody, who opened the first English-speaking kindergarten in Boston in 1860, and Mary Tyler Mann, widow of educator Horace Mann. Mary Mann helped Winnemucca get her book, *Life Among the Paiutes: Their Wrongs and Claims*, published in 1883. It was a best-seller.

In 1885, money from the sale of her book and from Peabody helped Winnemucca start the Peabody Indian School. Her goal was to teach Paiute students English while providing a basic education so they could teach others in the tribe. Winnemucca sang gospel songs in English to her class, then encouraged the students to repeat the songs. She believed that once the youngsters mastered the pronunciation, the meaning of the words would then be easier for students to grasp. In time, her ideas became the basis of a respected educational method known as phonics.

Because the Peabody Indian School did not teach about white culture, a requirement for government funding, it never received aid from the Indian Bureau. Winnemucca operated her school until 1889, when the Dawes Act made it a requirement that older Native American youngsters attend English-speaking boarding schools.

VARIETY IN EDUCATION

Innovations were taking place in the American university as well. One of the hot topics of discussion among professors and administrators was whether the classical curriculum should be varied. At Harvard, classical subjects—Latin, Greek, and mathematics—were standards; history, French, English, and German were not. There was strong faculty opposition when Harvard President Charles W. Eliot introduced the "free elective" system in 1868.

Eliot, the son of a wealthy Boston family, was a Harvard graduate who remembered feeling stifled by the course of study the college offered. He reasoned that because the country was known for its democracy, education should be made democratic as well by letting students choose what they wanted to learn. By 1894, a Harvard undergraduate could take a required number of courses in a variety of sub-

Education

Native American students hit the books at the Carlisle Indian School, which was run by the federal government.

jects, while studying English and a modern foreign language, and receive a Bachelor of Arts degree. In time, other institutions followed Harvard's lead. At the end of the century, Eliot had expanded the fields in which degrees were awarded at Harvard to include English, European and American history, physics, chemistry, and physiology.

An important social question at the turn of the century was how to help the immigrant population that was pouring into the cities. In most cases, parents had no choice but to leave their youngsters to fend for themselves in the slums and tenements while they worked to survive. Education of young children became part of the solution.

Margarethe Meyer Schurz is credited with initiating kindergarten in America. She operated the first kindergarten from her home in Watertown, Wisconsin, in 1857. Elizabeth Peabody started the first English-speaking kindergarten in Boston in 1860, and in 1873 Susan Blow set up the first public school kindergarten in St. Louis. Pauline Agassiz Shaw was instrumental in adding kindergartens to Boston's public school system, so that after 1890 the city's immigrant youngsters had a chance to experience a safe and nurturing learning environment.

Shaw was wealthy and prominent. Famed Harvard naturalist Louis Agassiz was her father; Elizabeth Cary Agassiz, the first president of Radcliffe College, was her stepmother; and her husband was copper mining heir Quincy Adams Shaw. Kindergartens became her passion, and she helped fund Peabody's work.

Shaw established charity kindergartens in Boston's North End, Jamaica Plain, and Brookline in 1870; by 1883 she had established 31 kindergartens and had convinced the Boston School Committee to hold two kindergarten classes in a local public school. She paid expenses for furniture, heat, and staff.

Children between 22 months and five years old were admitted to the

kindergarten program. After the youngsters entered the school, their faces were washed, their clothes were cleaned, and they sat down to a breakfast of milk and bread. Games were played and a rural theme was integrated into the program, with stories, drawings, and songs about nature. Shaw, however, also was aware of inner-city realities, and her program attempted to make parents take a hand in their children's progress. Mothers were invited to sit in on their children's classes, and parents were encouraged to meet the teachers at evening gatherings and learn about their methods. In an effort to win parents over, teachers visited the homes of both prospective and enrolled students.

By the mid-1880s, expenses had risen. Shaw spent over $200,000 on her schools between 1882 and 1889, and she began pressuring the Boston School Committee to take up the cause. It did in 1888 by adding 14 of Shaw's kindergartens to the city's public school system.

Overall, kindergartens were incorporated into most large public school systems as well as into the school districts of several suburbs and smaller cities by the turn of the century.

EDUCATION AND SOCIAL WORK

As the 19th century drew to a close, Americans began to develop a social conscience. Social work, as an organized way to help and advise the poor and less fortunate, was both a continuation and an outgrowth of education. Those who had decided to work in the field were now teaching skills, encouraging schooling, and sharing information so others' lives could improve. Janie Porter Barrett was so committed to her roles as educator and social worker that she founded the Locust Street Social Settlement in 1890, then, 25 years later, established a rehabilitation center for African-American girls who were in trouble with the law. Both projects were successful and received acclaim.

One of the most influential educators of the 19th and early 20th centuries, Charles W. Eliot (1834-1926) was president of Harvard University for 40 years. Under his guidance, the college elective system was developed and new courses were added, admissions standards and graduation requirements were raised, and the faculty was enlarged. Also, Eliot influenced the development of a more uniform high school curriculum.

Interestingly, Barrett's brilliant career began with a deeply personal dilemma: whether or not to pass for white in order to attend a northern school, which would be paid for by her mother's employer. The daughter of former slaves, she followed her mother's wishes and took classes at the Hampton Institute, a primarily black college in Hampton, Virginia.

Barrett went on to teach in the sharecropping town of Dawson,

37

Education

A class at the Hampton Institute in Virginia, which was one of the first colleges for blacks. The Institute also pioneered in Native American education.

Georgia, and later in Atlanta, before returning to the Hampton Institute to teach night classes. After marrying and bearing four children, she opened her home to aid and encourage people who were struggling. The opening of the Locust Street Social Settlement was a natural progression, and Barrett kept it running successfully by tapping the northern philanthropists she had met at Hampton Institute for funds. At the settlement house, people attended classes in sewing, caring for children, cooking, and raising livestock. In 1908, Barrett founded the Virginia State Federation of Colored Women's Clubs, and she encouraged the organization to become involved in social work.

Her work eventually led to an encounter with an eight-year-old girl who had been jailed, and the incident affected Barrett deeply. She believed the state needed a rehabilitation center, and her federation raised money to open the Virginia Industrial School for Colored Girls on a 147-acre farm 18 miles north of Richmond in 1915. Barrett lived at the school, which taught education and vocational skills to eight grades. Students who obeyed the rules were eligible for parole after two years. Those who left were placed in specially selected foster homes, and Barrett kept in touch with them.

The Virginia Industrial School for Colored Girls was unique in its time. There were no locks, bars, or physical punishment, and students were encouraged to raise grievances during an open forum. Barrett helped increase the school's enrollment to 100, initiated standards that set it apart from other institutions, and made it a respected example of what could occur when intelligence, commitment, caring, and funding meshed.

The Education
of American Women

"I DO NOT WANT TO SEE ONE SIDE OF LIFE ONLY, BUT MANY."
Ethel Waxham, the daughter of a prominent Denver physician, wrote
those words as a young woman over 100 years ago, voicing a yearn-
ing many women felt. From 1905 to 1909, Waxham got her wish. She
worked in a slum in a New York settlement house, taught school in
Hailey, Wyoming, earned a master's degree from the University of
Colorado, taught Latin at a girls' school in Kenosha, Wisconsin,
returned home to Denver to care for her father and half-sister, then
taught Latin in a Pueblo, Colorado, high school. Over the four-year
period, her adventures included a 125-mile overnight stagecoach ride
as well as sled commutes to school during blizzards.

Waxham was a 1905 graduate of Wellesley, one of the women's colleges that were booming at the turn of the century. These colleges
were an important development in the history of the country, as a
solution to the lack of higher education for women.

Emma Willard was one of many women who believed in the
necessity of education. Willard began a school in her home in

Mary Lyon (1797-1849) was interested in promoting higher education for women. She founded Mount Holyoke Female Seminary in 1837 and developed a program emphasizing service to others.

Middlebury, Vermont, in 1814, and later she composed a letter to the New York State Legislature asking for state aid in establishing female seminaries. When town administrators in Troy, New York, approached her about establishing a training school for women teachers with women overseers, she jumped at the chance. Her Troy Female Seminary, founded in 1821, started an enduring educational network. Over 12,000 women attended the seminary over the next 50 years, and many established schools of their own.

Others who founded teaching schools during the 1820s and '30s were Catherine Beecher, in Hartford, Connecticut; Zilpha Grant, in Ipswich,

Massachusetts; and Mary Lyon, in South Hadley, Massachusetts. Their schools had high standards and encouraged creative thought, and the founders were passionate about education. Mount Holyoke, Lyon's South Hadley school, became a college in 1885. Lyon encouraged close ties between teacher and student, and the school's original building was constructed like a large home, with over 100 students and teachers living and learning in the same building. Mount Holyoke students were made to feel they had an important mission: to educate.

These teaching academies had a domino effect. Inspired graduates, who had been exposed to a new way of thinking and believed they could make a difference, taught all over the country. During the 1840s, for example, several hundred graduates from Catherine Beecher's academy were sent west to frontier towns that didn't have schools. These alumni traveled hundreds of miles by railroad. Then they scrambled onto boats that sailed over lakes, rivers, and canals, finishing their journeys in jostling, dusty stagecoaches. Once at their destinations, the women lived alone and were faced with many challenging decisions and situations.

In many other ways, American women were becoming more independent during this time. Many women came together in 1850 for the first national women's rights conference in Worcester, Massachusetts. Women began giving public lectures and were working in new fields. Also by this time, Elizabeth Blackwell had become the first American woman to earn her medical degree. Blackwell started the New York Infirmary for Women and Children with her sister, Emily, and Dr. Marie Zakrzewska, in 1857.

DEVELOPMENT OF WOMEN'S COLLEGES

As women became more visible in the workplace and in leadership

The campus of Vassar College as it appeared when it opened in 1865. One of the "Seven Sisters" colleges for women, the school was a leading institution of higher education. Vassar became coeducational in 1968.

roles, and immigrants continued to enter America by the thousands, an urgent need for teachers arose. Also, the loss of life in the Civil War created many single-parent households. By the end of the Civil War, there were only three coeducational colleges, not enough to accommodate the growing female population that needed education. In addition to these social conditions, there were many women—the daughters of the emerging middle-class families—who felt that access to higher educa-

A $400,000 grant from Matthew Vassar, who owned a brewery in Poughkeepsie, New York, endowed Vassar College in 1861.

tion for women shouldn't be an issue. This set the stage for the founding of women's colleges.

Interestingly, Matthew Vassar, the Poughkeepsie, New York, brewer who funded the first American college for women in 1861, was not initially an advocate for women's education. A self-made man who never attained a college degree, Vassar had the satisfaction of a successful career and a lot of money, and he could not decide whether to endow a hospital, a library, a boys' school, or some other worthy organization. At the urging of educator Milo Jewett, he invested $400,000 in a women's college.

Earlier, Jewett had founded the Judson Female Institute in Marion, Alabama. When his anti-slavery beliefs forced him to move north, he purchased a small school for girls in Poughkeepsie, which was later run by Vassar's niece. Jewett became friends with Vassar and suggested

funding a college when Vassar asked for advice.

Jewett had plans of his own and wanted to be president of the first endowed college for women. He never was, because of a falling-out with his benefactor, but by this time Vassar was totally committed to a new college for women. The school was a liberal arts college with emphasis on the fine arts and natural sciences. Vassar College opened in 1865 with a full faculty that included Maria Mitchell, who had discovered a new comet in 1847 and was the first woman to join the prestigious American Academy of Arts and Sciences. Mitchell was given her own building—the Vassar College Observatory was built for her as a home, laboratory, and classroom. However, the other important teaching positions went to men.

The Sophia Smith College, now known as Smith College, opened 10 years after Vassar, in 1875. It was named after its founder, Sophia Smith, who inherited a vast fortune from her brother. The new school's benefactor was similar to Matthew Vassar, because she had no previous association with either education or women's groups. Her minister, John Greene, was an advocate of women's education, and tried to persuade Smith to endow Mount Holyoke, 10 miles away, or his alma mater, Amherst College, but she rejected these suggestions. When Greene proposed funding the first women's college in New England, Smith agreed.

While Vassar was located in a rural setting, Smith was built near the center of Northampton, Massachusetts, a bustling town. Its students were housed on campus, like Vassar, but instead of residing in one building, they lived in one-floor cottages. Smith College had a male president and a female principal.

Sophia Smith was an eccentric, shy woman who had been kept under the thumb of her controlling brother for many years. Although

Howard University in Washington, D.C., was established to train young African-American women to teach.

initially she hadn't wanted to give $300,000 to a women's college, when the decision was made she was specific about the school's vision. Smith College would offer a way for women to develop the skills and intellectual power that previously had been denied them. She wanted Smith students to have a full curriculum in a liberal arts program that included ancient languages and mathematics. Lab sciences and geology trips also became part of Smith's program.

Unlike Vassar and Smith, where men held the top faculty positions, women filled all staff positions at Wellesley, including the office of president. The school was founded by Henry Durant as a women's seminary in Boston and became a college in 1875. Alice Freeman Palmer, who took over as president in 1881, was a genius at organization and gave the school its identity. She raised Wellesley's standards, simplified course offerings, added math, Latin, vocal, and drawing requirements, and initiated a variety of electives. Christianity was emphasized, and Palmer felt a student's social and moral progress was just as important as her intellectual development.

While Wellesley evolved into a desirable college for women, there were attractions for teachers as well. Harvard chemistry professor Eben Horsford, who made a fortune from a baking soda formula, paid for an elegant faculty room where professors could sit and relax, and he opened his Maine summer home to vacationing staff. He also funded a one-year sabbatical in Europe for senior faculty and established a pension fund.

The "Seven Sisters" colleges—Mount Holyoke, Vassar, Smith, Wellesley, Radcliffe, Bryn Mawr, and Barnard—all admitted women by 1889. Unfortunately, while the schools did create opportunities for women, not everyone was eligible. At first, only white Protestant women were allowed to attend. By the end of the century, there was a

In 1886, Josephine Newcomb donated $100,000 to help fund a college for women in New Orleans. Newcomb College, which was associated with Tulane University, became the first women's institution for higher learning in the South.

tiny enrollment of Catholics and Jews. Wellesley accepted black students, and it was the only college in this group that didn't discriminate in admissions or housing.

In the South, Newcomb College became the first women's institution for higher learning in 1886. Josephine Newcomb, who lived part of each year in New Orleans, donated $100,000 to fund the college, which was associated with all-male Tulane University. Newcomb, which started with a physical education program, became known for its high standards and its art department, and like the "Seven Sisters" it is still a thriving institution.

While higher educational choices were limited for black women, there were universities that had been established to train African Americans to teach. Howard University in Washington, D.C., Morehouse College in Atlanta, Fisk University in Nashville, and the Hampton Institute had already been established by 1869. Ohio's Oberlin College had been operating as a coeducational college, open to women and African Americans, since its founding in 1833.

Between 1870 and 1890, over 1,000 female college graduates would become teachers. There also were about a dozen who became doctors, and many went on to become nurses, librarians, and editors. Susan LaFlesche Picotte graduated from the Women's Medical College of Philadelphia in 1889, the first Native American to receive a medical degree. She went on to treat Omaha tribe members and eventually became a leader of the tribe.

Women who would become prominent and influential were emerging from these colleges and entering many areas, including social work, art, the literary world, architecture, and journalism. By 1900, there were 85,000 female college students, representing 35 percent of the nation's college population.

Improving Education
Through Reform

YEARS AFTER KATHERINE PETTIT OPENED THE COUNTRY'S first rural settlement school in Hindman, Kentucky, followed by a sister settlement in nearby Pine Mountain, she received a letter from a former student saying, "You always did hit straight from the shoulder, Miss Pettit." What Pettit "hit" was an effective way to integrate local Appalachian skills, like farming, cooking, and furniture making, with reading, writing, and arithmetic.

Her journey began when an 82-year-old Kentucky resident asked Pettit and colleague May Stone to "come to larn the young 'uns." Rolling up their sleeves, Pettit and Stone pitched a tent overlooking a creek in Knott County, Kentucky, to teach the children of the area. Although the locals thought the pair was strange, youngsters came daily in significant numbers to what became the Hindman Settlement School.

Pettit and Stone, and later Ethel de Long, who with Pettit started the Pine Mountain school, were among a legion of settlement school founders, teaching basic life skills and academic subjects while encour-

Settlement schools, like this one in the Oklahoma Territory circa 1895, taught the children of local farmers and ranchers important skills like cooking and furniture making, along with reading, writing, and arithmetic.

aging each region's culture. Settlement school workers lived in the community to learn firsthand what its residents needed for successful lives, then offered courses or services to match those needs. As a result, many people gained a chance for education, personal growth, and a satisfying, independent life. It was a unique, much-needed approach, and as a result there were over 400 of these settlement schools by 1910.

Between 1865 and 1914, millions of immigrants arrived in America. Many settled in urban areas like New York, Boston, and Philadelphia. Educating the immigrant children was a challenge because many spoke no English, only the language of the country where their parents were born.

THE PROBLEM OF CHILD LABOR

The settlement houses were among the many reforms that addressed the educational inequities and problems of the time. One major concern was child labor. Although 31 states and territories had compulsory

53

school attendance laws by the turn of the century, the rules were not strictly enforced and about two million children were in the workforce. It would take some time for attitudes to begin shifting.

The main reasons for child labor were economic. Business owners who hired youngsters to work in their factories and mills could pay low wages and earn larger profits. At the same time, many immigrant families felt they had no choice but to send their children to work so the family could survive.

The National Child Labor Committee, founded in 1905, sought to change the nation's attitude toward child labor. Headed by Dr. Felix Adler, the committee issued articles by its investigators, who reported what they observed in factories, canneries, and farms. It was not until 1907, when Lewis Hine began chronicling young workers in photographs for the committee, that the nation's conscience was awakened. Hine had to sneak into businesses in order to record the working conditions, because business owners opposed the committee's work. His tireless investigation and interviews resulted in stories and illustrations that captured the unsafe, difficult conditions. Hine made his photos into slides and showed them at conferences and exhibits around the country. By 1916, the first federal law was passed that regulated child labor. That legislation, the Keating-Owen Act, made it illegal to ship goods produced by children across state lines.

On the other hand, for immigrant children new to America, facing a classroom for the first time could be positively bewildering. To help ease their way, educators like New York School Superintendent William H. Maxwell initiated "steamer classes," six-month English courses for non-English-speaking students, in 1910. These courses gave immigrant children a chance to learn the language of their new country and helped remove some of the disadvantages these children experi-

The new arrivals in the United States were crowded into small tenement apartments. An education was necessary to help immigrant youths move out of these urban slums.

Education

Without specific industrial skills, young men who did not go on to college usually ended up in low-wage, dead-end jobs. To equip students like these with the skills they needed to earn a living when they grew older, schools began incorporating technical training into the curriculum around the turn of the century.

enced as newcomers. Previously all immigrant children had been placed in first grade, regardless of their age. At the same time, a private New York group called the Penny Lunch Committee offered these children nutritious lunches for one penny.

An important service initiated as a way to help students having difficulty in school was the visiting teacher movement, which also started in New York. The influential Public Education Association of New York City, formed by the Junior League and women who wanted to improve public schools, organized and funded this new service in 1907. Teachers met with youngsters having difficulty in school, and visited their parents, both to get a sense of their home life and to plan projects with the family to help the student. Teachers then reported each child's specific needs to school officials.

These visiting teachers spent a lot of time with the students. For example, if a child had a talent for music, the teacher encouraged the school to help the youth demonstrate that talent whenever possible. Sometimes children with a learning problem were afraid or embarrassed to tell the teacher, so gaining trust was important. At times, the teacher had to make several decisions to solve a student's problems. In one particular case, a 14-year-old girl was failing because her family had pressured her to provide income. The father of this newly arrived immigrant family was dead, the mother was sickly, and the girl's brother did not have a job, so the teen sold small items after school. This was a violation of the law, but to really help the student, the teacher would have to find a job for the brother. Also, the girl would need some personal attention so that she would see another aspect of life in America and aspire to succeed in school.

African Americans benefitted from a similar service. Visiting teachers, funded at first by the Anna Jeannes Fund and later by the Phelps

Stokes Fund, began traveling to the South's rural areas to instruct black teachers in industrial methods so they could pass this training on to students. Later, intellectual learning would be encouraged as well.

MATCHING EDUCATION AND INDUSTRY

The fate of high school graduates also became an important concern to the public school system. Although schools provided the basics, many students would not go to college and would work at industrial jobs. Without specific training, they were destined to hold low-wage, dead-end positions.

A 1906 report, sponsored by the Massachusetts Commission on Industrial and Technical Education, kicked off the vocational guidance movement. The report included interviews with parents, school super-intendents and principals, and the employers of the 14- and 15-year-old students who had left schools for industrial jobs. The report concluded that state public schools were not equipping students for employment. To be successful, these students needed access to technical training.

Germany's education system was used as an example. That country was a rising world power, and many people believed Germany's industrial success could be traced to its mandatory vocational and technical schools for those who were not college-bound. If Massachusetts wanted to help its students, and in turn its own economy, it would need to introduce manual training at all levels and change schools' cultural thrust, funding vocational and technical high schools in every large town, the report stated.

To accomplish this, a school agency was established. In 1908, Frank Parsons, who is usually credited with starting the vocational guidance movement, founded the Vocation Bureau in Boston. Its staff would meet with high school students and guide them toward their futures.

The typical elementary school classroom of the early 20th century. The teacher is explaining Native American history and lore to her students.

Pauline Agassiz Shaw, the city's great educational philanthropist and kindergarten initiator, funded the bureau.

Within a few months after the Vocation Bureau opened, counselors paid by the city's public schools were being trained. Their task was to decide which elementary school graduates should attend the city's technical high schools. The theory quickly spread to other parts of the country. Two years later, when the first National Conference on Vocational Guidance was held in Boston, delegates from 45 cities attended.

ADDRESSING IMMIGRANTS' NEEDS

While the settlement and vocational schools were trying to address the educational needs of their communities, an organization started in 1910 specifically assisted new and second-generation immigrant women and children. Called the International Institute, and sponsored by the Young Women's Christian Association, it was founded in New York by Edith Terry Bremer, a social worker. The organization offered English classes, recreational and club activities, information about citizenship, and help finding a place to live and a job. Other International Institutes were established in Trenton, New Jersey; Los Angeles; Pittsburgh; and Lawrence, Massachusetts, within five years.

Bremer was a graduate of the University of Chicago and spent time as a social worker, a field investigator for the Chicago Juvenile Court, a researcher for the Chicago Women's Trade Union League, and a special agent for the United States Immigration Commission before she started the Institutes. She traveled and set up new Institutes, visited each to review programs, and organized annual meetings. She also was passionate about championing the immigrants and their value to the nation, and she stamped her philosophy on the Institutes that she organized. Cultures and traditions were treated with respect, and her

For many immigrant children, the first English they learned was the words to the Pledge of Allegiance.

movement emphasized the similarities, not the differences, in the human race. Bremer believed the quest to "Americanize" everyone was wrong, and she fought for favorable immigrant legislation.

Courses at the Institutes included English, American history, and government, as well as practical subjects like health care. Because of Bremer's vision, ethnic programs in language, history, literature, and other areas were offered as well, and ethnic festivals were organized. The Institute also scheduled foreign-born speakers to discuss topics of interest to the immigrants. Bremer retired as executive director of the renamed American Federation of International Institutes in 1953.

How the Universities Developed

LIFE WAS VERY DIFFERENT ON THE AVERAGE SMALL college campus before the Civil War. Everyone knew each other, because there were fewer than 100 students and only a handful of teachers. Applicants didn't have to worry about the Scholastic Assessment Test (SAT), but knowledge of Latin, Greek, and math were required for enrollment. No one dashed to class because campus grounds were small—usually a couple of buildings overlooking an open quadrangle. There were no lines at the registrar's office, because only one curriculum was offered, including classical languages, math, natural sciences, moral philosophy, and history. Lively, thought-provoking classes probably occurred, but for the most part students learned through memorization and recitation.

The American workforce was focusing on industry. Knowledge of Latin and Greek, while valuable, didn't address the technical and scientific problems the country faced: how to build safe, high structures or more powerful engines, or how to cure various diseases. Apprenticeships with a master craftsman had for centuries been a successful

Congressman Justin S. Morrill created legislation that allowed the states to fund higher education through the sale of federally owned property. These "land-grant colleges" offered programs in agriculture, engineering, and home economics, as well as traditional academic subjects.

way to teach skills, but they were not practical anymore.

At this time, there were a few technical colleges, like New York State's Agricultural College. Congressman Justin Smith Morrill of Vermont wanted a more varied learning experience, and he began pushing for educational institutions that offered liberal and practical education in several professions. In 1858, he proposed that 30,000 acres of land be deeded to each state senator and representative. Money from the sale of this real estate would then be set aside to support at least one college for practical education.

The bill did not draw immediate support; it was five years before the bill was signed into law by President Abraham Lincoln in 1862. Even after its passage, the concept wasn't accepted right away. For example, New Hampshire, Pennsylvania, Connecticut, and Illinois reported very little student interest when their land grant institutions opened. However, by the end of the century, 69 land-grant colleges were established across the United States.

Many other colleges grew and thrived during this period. The concept of a modern American university—one institution with several professional colleges offering different degrees on campus grounds—began with Cornell University in 1868. Endowed by Ezra Cornell, who added $500,000 of his personal fortune to the land grant funds, Cornell became a coed university that offered degrees in science, the humanities, engineering, and agriculture. Its programs were so popular that the university attracted the country's largest freshman class ever in just its third year.

In 1754, King's College was founded in New York through a grant from England's King George II. It was renamed Columbia College in 1784 and became Columbia University in 1896, when it moved uptown to its present campus in Morningside Heights. Early Columbia students

Tuskegee Institute, a school for educating African Americans, was founded in Alabama in 1881. Under Booker T. Washington, who organized the school, Tuskegee became one of the leading black educational institutions. Industrial training in various fields was emphasized. These students are working in the school's printing shop around 1909.

like Hugh Auchincloss Brown, class of 1900, remembered horse cars, elevated railroads, and no pollution surrounding this city university.

Seth Low, Columbia's president from 1890 to 1901, was responsible for changing the institution from a college to a university. Low also initiated paid sabbatical leave, which allowed professors time for research. By 1909, Columbia had become a leader in summer-session enrollment, a concept first introduced at the University of Chicago. In that year, Columbia boasted over 1,900 summer-session students—two-thirds from other schools.

Some universities actually tried to find solutions to social problems. The University of Wisconsin was among the first, offering courses that addressed community needs. Behind the leadership of university president John Bascom, in 1877 Wisconsin began offering short agricultural courses and research programs devoted to the problems of the state's dairy industry. By the end of the century, Wisconsin had added schools of economics, political science, and history to prepare students for administrative roles in the state's civil service. Other state schools, like the universities of Michigan and Illinois, followed Wisconsin's example.

To educate African Americans granted freedom after the Civil War, about 200 private and church-supported colleges were founded between 1870 and 1890. Although these schools were intended to provide an education for blacks that equalled that of whites, most were underfunded. Howard University and Fisk University were two that offered a course of study similar to that of a good liberal arts university. Philanthropists who could be counted on to support black education leaned toward practical job training over a classical curriculum, supporting schools like the Hampton Institute or the Tuskegee Institute, which was founded by Booker T. Washington in 1881. Nine African-American institutions of higher learning were founded in the South

through land-grant appropriations by 1890. In that year, a second Morrill Act was passed specifically to improve African-American education, and the South gained 17 black land-grant colleges.

Also during this time, more students continued their education after college. By the 1870s, research-based graduate universities emerged with the establishment of Johns Hopkins in Baltimore, which based its

continued on page 73

One of the earliest institutes of higher learning in the American colonies was King's College. The college was granted a charter in 1754 by King George II of England. Although the school closed during the Revolutionary War and this building was used by American soldiers, after the war the college was reopened and renamed Columbia College. Now known as Columbia University, it is located in the heart of New York City.

Many of the Puritans who settled in America during the 17th century were graduates of Oxford or Cambridge universities in England. They wanted to ensure that a good education would be available in the colonies for their children, so in 1636 the General Court of Massachusetts voted to raise money for a new college. The school was named for a young minister who was dying of tuberculosis, John Harvard. He donated his 400-book library and half of his money to the new college.

YALE COLLEGE.

Yale University was the third college established in the American colonies, after Harvard and the College of William and Mary. Yale was founded in 1701 and originally was known as the Collegiate School. The college moved to New Haven, where it is currently located, in 1716.

The College of William and Mary was the first college established in Virginia. The honor fraternity Phi Beta Kappa was started at William and Mary in 1776, and in 1779 the college instituted an elective system of study, similar to that of modern colleges and universities. Alumni of William and Mary, which was founded in 1693, include three former presidents: Thomas Jefferson, James Monroe, and John Tyler.

continued from page 68

programs on the German system of the Doctor of Philosophy (Ph.D.) degree as its highest award. Johns Hopkins was unique in offering specific post-college studies. There were 13 graduate departments, along with undergraduate classes, and it had a first-class medical school. Because of the demand for higher education, students flocked to Johns Hopkins, which graduated more Ph.D.s in the next two decades than Harvard and Yale combined. Together, the three advanced educational programs had lured over 5,000 graduate students nationally by 1900.

STUDENT LIFE

The students attending these universities weren't that different from the students of today. Sometimes they disrupted class with activities like unified foot-stomping. At Princeton University, students brought alarm clocks to lecture halls, setting them so they would ring at various intervals. Although there were many good-natured pranks, there also were incidents of bias, bigotry, and elitism. There was bitterness about women being included on some campuses that had been male-only, and some students were shunned because of their name, race, or appearance.

For over 100 years, one of the major passions associated with university and student life has been football. The first intercollegiate game took place when Princeton and Rutgers played on Nov. 6, 1869, with 25 men on each team. The game resembled soccer more than modern American football, and Rutgers won, six goals to four. Weekend games began in 1881, when a Michigan team traveled east to play Harvard, Princeton, and Yale. By 1883, cities like New York were caught up in the football spirit. Fifth Avenue mansions were decorated with Yale and Princeton colors, and local pastors cut their sermons short to attend games. Football became a way for schools to receive valuable publicity,

and many universities latched on quickly. It also kept alumni connected to their schools and fostered school spirit.

Unfair practices and deadly injuries in college sports were common at first. The fatality rate for football injuries reached 18 in the 1905 season, with over 100 students seriously injured. To help a team win, coaches paid "ringers," or athletes who weren't students, to play for their teams. The fatalities, injuries, and corrupt practices caused an uproar, and a White House conference on organized sports took place, prompting the formation of what became known as the National College Athletic Association (NCAA). This intercollegiate association helped set standards for safe, honest athletic contests.

Women's athletics made their debut at this time as well, and sports such as track, crew, and swimming were pursued on some campuses. Women's basketball had just been initiated at Smith College when Senda Berenson, a physical education teacher, listed the "Basketball Rules for Women" in 1892. Later, in 1905, Berenson served as chair of the basketball rules committee for the American Association for the Advent of Physical Education. According to her rules, players could dribble only three times and hold the ball for just three seconds. Women's basketball teams from the University of California at Berkeley and Stanford University played the first intercollegiate game in 1896.

SETTING ACADEMIC STANDARDS

While an effort to set standards for sports was taking place, university administrators felt the time had come to do the same with academics. Perhaps only about 20 percent of the country's 700 universities and colleges had solid academic programs at the turn of the century. The discrepancies varied. In some cases, professors wrestled with a heavy weekly teaching schedule. At other schools, a high school diploma was

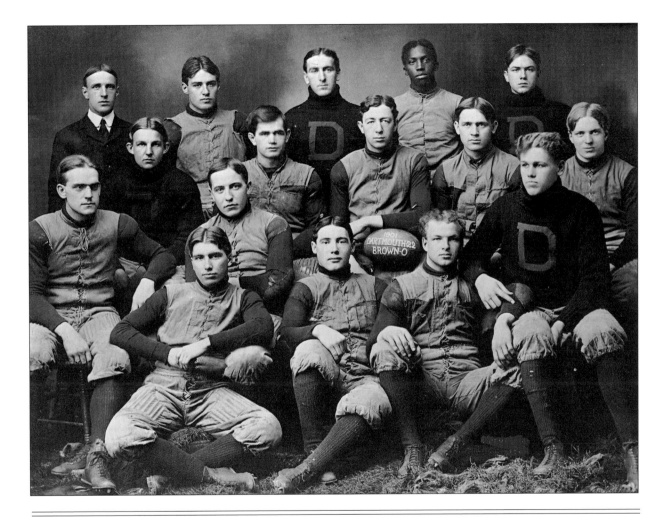

College football was vastly different 100 years ago. Players wore minimal padding and no helmets, and the game focused more on running than passing. This is Dartmouth College's 1901 team.

The classroom is certainly a different place today than it was for these students around 1900. However, the primary focus of education remains the same: to provide children with the skills they will need in their adult lives.

the only requirement for admission.

In 1900, presidents and deans at a dozen of the leading graduate universities of the day founded the Association of American Universities in an attempt to address these inequities. The goal was to create a uniform system of Ph.D. requirements, to obtain recognition and respect for Ph.D. programs in America, and to help raise the standards of less-credible universities. The association eventually became an accrediting agency.

Professional standards were becoming issues, and it was just a matter of time before professors banded together. The American Association of University Professors, founded in 1915, set standards for teachers. Academic freedom was another concern for professors. There were many cases of teachers who were fired because they expressed a belief or philosophy in their classes that was not in tune with school administrators' beliefs.

Another organization, the American Association of University Women (AAUW) developed during this period. Ellen Swallow Richards, a scientist who helped establish a women's laboratory at the Massachusetts Institute of Technology, cofounded a group in 1888 that disproved the theory that education damaged a woman's health. This group gradually developed into the AAUW. The organization's goal, which it still holds today, was to promote the advancement of women at the nation's universities and colleges.

The evolution of higher education, the development of learning opportunities for everyone, and the many reforms and improvements in education at the turn of the century were the basis of today's American education system. New methods of transportation, growing cities, and the movement from an agricultural to an industrial nation each were changes that affected how Americans lived and worked, and

education was affected by these forces as well. Although the subjects students learn, and the way in which these subjects are taught, are very different from the methods of 100 years ago, the basic function of education remains the same: to provide everyone with the skills needed for a happy and productive life.

FURTHER READING

Alan Brinkley, et al. *American History: A Survey-Vol. 2*. New York: McGraw-Hill Inc., 1991.

Church, Robert L. *Education in the United States*. New York: The Free Press, 1976.

Curti, Merle. *The Growth of American Thought*. New York: Harper & Row Publishers, 1964.

DeJong, David H. *Promises of the Past: A History of Indian Education*. Golden, Colo.: North American Press, 1993.

Evans, Sara M. *Born For Liberty: A History of Women in America*. New York: The Free Press, 1989.

First, Wesley, ed. *University on the Heights*. New York: Doubleday & Co., Inc., 1969.

Frankfort, Roberta. *Collegiate Women*. New York: University Press, 1977.

Furnas, J.C. *The Americans: A Social History of the United States 1587-1914*. New York: G.P. Putnam's Sons, 1969.

Gehman, Mary, and Nancy Ries. *Women and New Orleans*. New Orleans: Margaret Media Inc., 1988.

Geiger, Roger L. *To Advance Knowledge: The Growth of American Research Universities 1900-1940*. New York: Oxford University Press, 1986.

Hofstadter, Richard, and Walter Metzger. *The Development of Academic Freedom in the United States*. New York: Columbia University Press, 1955.

Kaplan, Daile. *Lewis Hine in Europe: The Lost Photographs*. New York: Abbeville Press, 1988.

Katz, Michael B., ed. *Education in American History: Readings on the Social Issues*. New York: Praeger Publishers, 1973.

Kendall, Elaine. *Peculiar Institutions: An Informal History of the Seven Sister Colleges*. New York: G.P. Putnam's Sons, 1975.

Lacour-Gayet, Robert. *Everyday Life in the United States Before the Civil War 1830-1860*. New York: Frederick Ungar Publishing Co., 1969.

Love, Barbara, and Frances Love Froidevaux. *Lady's Choice: Ethel Waxham's Journals and Letters 1905-1910*. Albuquerque: University of New Mexico Press, 1993.

Lucas, Christopher. *American Higher Education: A History*. New York: St. Martin's Press, 1994.

Matthews, Glenna. *The Rise of Public Woman: Woman's Power and Woman's Place in the United States 1630-1970*. New York: Oxford University Press, 1992.

Miller, Page Putnam, ed. *Reclaiming the Past: Landmarks of Women's History*. Bloomington, Ind.: Indiana University Press, 1992.

Read, Phyllis J., and Bernard L. Witlieb. *The Book of Women's Firsts*. New York: Random House, 1992.

Sherr, Lynn, and Jurate Kazickas. *Susan B. Anthony Slept Here: A Guide to American Women's Landmarks*. New York: Times Books, 1994.

Sigerman, Harriet. *Laborers for Liberty: American Women 1865-1890*. New York: Oxford University Press, 1994.

Smith, William A. *Ancient Education*. New York: Philosophical Library, 1955.

Weiss, Bernard J., ed. *American Education and the European Immigrant 1840-1940*. Chicago: University of Illinois Press, 1982.

INDEX

PICTURE CREDITS

LINDA LEUZZI has written several volumes for the Life in America 100 Years Ago series, including *Transportation, Urban Life*, and *Industry and Business*. Her other books include *A Matter of Style: Women in the Fashion Industry* and *To the Young Environmentalist*, and her articles have appeared in *New York Newsday, Family Circle, Ladies' Home Journal, Weight Watchers*, and *New Woman*. She is a member of the American Society of Journalists and Authors and the Newswomen's Club of New York.

ghly, very durably
de. Weight, packed, 4
nces. Each 6c.

Per doz............................$0.65
Per gross.......................6.95

**53510 The Matchless
Dustless Eraser,** made of thin
fancy colored felt, firmly
secured, forming a substantial and perfect eraser.
Each......................$0.05

Per doz......................55
Per gross....................5.45

outh's Com-
anion and Re-
ersible Black-
board.

53512 **Combination
riting and Drawing
sk.** Suitable for
me, Sunday and
vate schools. Both
slated, hard wood
me. 3 feet 11 inches
2 feet wide. The
st complete, perfect
d reliable black board
de. Price..... $3.00

Portable Black-Boards.

**53514 Port-
able Blackboard**
of cloth with best
black liquid slat-
ing surface on
both sides,
mounted on roll-
ers with hook and
rings complete

hanging.

Size.	Each.	Size.	Each.	Size.	Each.
ft.	$0 54	3x5 ft.	$1 90	4x5 ft.	$2 30
ft.	1 14	3x6 ft.	2 30	4x6 ft.	2 85
ft.	1 50	4x4 ft.	1 90	4x7 ft.	3 50

With music lines, $1.25 each, additional.

**3516 Portable
ackboard** of Hylo-
te, slated both sides;
th ash frame; for
e on wall, easel or
le.

ft..................	$2.60	3½x5	$5.50
ft..................	3.60	4 x6	7.15
½ ft................	4.55		

With music lines, $1.25 each additional.
Reversible portable blackboards, same as No.
6, mounted on hardwood standards, for private
ools, Sunday schools, lecture rooms, etc. Prices
l be quoted on application.

Slated Paper and Cloth.

3518 **For Blackboard; excellent for any flat
rface.** Per yard.
aper, 3 ft. wide, slated one side, black...... $0.47
aper, 4 ft. wide, slated one side, black...... .60
3520
loth, 3 ft. wide, slated one side, black...... .54
loth, 4 ft. wide, slated one side, black...... .67
loth, 3 ft. wide, slated two sides, black...... .67
loth, 4 ft. wide, slated two sides, black...... .80

iquid Slating for Blackboards.

3522 **Best Alcohol Black Liquid Slating:** may

Bound School Slates combine
strength, lightness, durability, and
uniformity of finish of surface; being
wire bound, they cannot come apart,
and machine smoothed they present
an absolutely even writing surface,
free from ridges.

Size.	Each.	Per doz.	Wt., Ea.
6x 9........................	$0.04	$0.42	18 oz.
7x11........................	0.05	0.48	22 oz.
8x12........................	0.06	0.60	25 oz.
6x 9, 12 doz. in case, per case...			$4.75
7x11, 10 doz. in case, per case...			4.50
8x12, 8 doz. in case, per case...			4.50

"Hyatt Noiseless Slates.

53528 **Strength, lightness
and durability combined.**
Best quality slate with perfectly finished, even writing surface, free from ridges. Frame
is wire bound (cannot come
apart) and covered with fine
bright red (fast color) wool felt,
securely fastened.
"Hyatt" Noiseless Slate,
single.

Size.	Each.	Per doz.	Wt., Ea.
6x 9........................	$0.08	$0.80	18 oz.
7x11........................	0.10	1.00	23 oz.
8x12........................	0.12	1.20	26 oz.
6x 9, 12 doz. in case, per case...			$9.00
7x11, 10 doz. in case, per case...			9.00
8x12, 8 doz. in case, per case...			8.40

53529 **"Hyatt" Noiseless Slate,** double, hinged
with strong webbing, firmly riveted to frames.

Size.	Each.	Per doz.	Wt., Ea.
7x11........................	$0.20	$2.00	40 oz.
8x12........................	0.24	2.40	46 oz.
7x11, 5 doz. in case, per case...			$9.00
8x12, 4 doz. in case...			8.40

Victor Slates.

53530 **Best Quality Slates,**
with perfectly smooth surface;
frame covered with bright red
wool felt and securely fastened.

Size.	Each.	Per doz.
5x7.....	$0.08	$0.80
6x9..............	.09	.95
7x11.............	.10	1.05
8x12.............	.12	1.25

Silicate Book Slates.

Superior
quality, strongly made, bound in
fine black cloth covers. Superior
slate surface for the slate pencil.
For school or office use.

Size.	Each.
53532 6 surfaces....5x8½	$0.25
6 surfaces....6x9	.35

Silicate Book Slates, neatly and
strongly bound in fine cloth, with
superior **ivorine surface, for the**
lead pencil. For the pocket.
53534 6 surfaces, size 3x5, each.............. $0.15
10 surfaces, size 3¼x5½, each.......... .25

Scholar's Companions.

53413 **Turned Wood
Case,** fancy paper cov-
ered, furnished with slate
and lead pencil, pen
holder and ruler. Each, 3c; per doz.......... $0.30

53415 **Unique Scholar's
Companion,** varnished maple box, with sliding cover,
9-inch ruler attachment with scale, fitted with lead
pencil, slate pencil and pen holder. Size, 9x2x1⅛
inches. Each, 8c; per doz.................. $0.85

5341_ _ _
ar's C_
bass wood, shel_
lac_ _ _
partments each

---

ceipts, invoices, let-
ters and memoranda
of every description,
made from best
spring steel and brass
double length.
53473. **"Ever-
Handy" Paper Clip,**
small size, with jaws
1¼ inches wide,
Each $0.04
Per dozen....... 0.40
53474. **"Ever-
Handy" Paper Clip,** medium size, with jaw_
inches wide. Each..$0.06 Per doz..........

"Spencerian" Ever-Hand_
Paper Clip.

53475. **"Spencerian" Paper C_**
Horseshoe shape; brass, size 1¾
inches.
Each......................
Per dozen...................

School Bags.

53490. **School Bag.** Fa_
Hemp, embroidered front, _
pocket; size 11½ x 14 in_
weight packed 5 oz.
Each.......................
Per doz....................

53491. **Waterproof School
Bag,** with outside pocket, shoul-
der strap and flap, bound edges.
Weight packed 5 oz.
Each, 14 in..... .... $.10
Per doz................... .95
Each, 16 inch............ .12
Per doz.................. 1.20

53492. **School Bag,** _
cotton cord, closely wove_
variegated colored stri_
lined, cord handles, 14 inc_
Each....................$_
Per doz.................

53493. **School Bag,**
Brown Duck, flap fastens
with strap and lock, leather
shoulder strap. Size 9½x14.
Very durable.
Each................. $0.18
Per doz............. 1.90

53494 **School Bags,** cot_
cord in variegated colo_
stripes, lined with colored c_
bric, with drawing strings,
when open 14x17½ inches.
Each....................$_
Per dozen... .... _

53495 **Book Straps,** flexible leather, handle w_
_ me plate, 36 inch strap.
..................................$_
Per doz_